Plant Life Cycles

Anita Ganeri

Heinemann Library
Chicago, Illinois

2005 Heinemann Library
an imprint of Capstone Global Library, LLC
Chicago, Illinois

Customer Service 888-454-2279

Visit our website at www.heinemannlibrary.com

Designed by Jo Malivoire
Printed in the United States of America in Eau Claire, Wisconsin.   042013   007359R

15 14 13 12 11
10 9 8 7

Library of Congress Cataloging-in-Publication Data
Ganeri, Anita, 1961-
   Plant life cycles / Anita Ganeri.
      p. cm. — (Nature's patterns)
   Includes bibliographical references and index.
   ISBN 1-4034-5896-0 ((hc)) — ISBN 1-4109-1319-8 ((pbk.))
   ISBN 978-1-4034-5896-4 ((hc)) — ISBN 978-1-4109-1319-7 ((pbk.))
   1. Plant life cycles—Juvenile literature. I. Title. II. Series.
   QK49.G339 2004
   571.8'2—dc22
                                    2004007465

Acknowledgments
The author and publishers are grateful to the following for permission to reproduce copyright
material: pp. **4**, **5**, **14**, **16**, **18**, **19**, **22**, **23**, **27** Photodisc; p. 6 Dr. Eckart Pott/NHPA; p. **7**, **26**
Ernie Janes/ NHPA; pp. **8**, **30** Cumulus; pp. **10**, **12** Holt Studios International/Cumulus; pp. **11**,
24 Harcourt; p. **15** OSF; p. **17** George Bernard/NHPA; p. **20** Getty; p. **21** Corbis; p. **25** James
Warwick/NHPA; p. **28** Holt Studios/International/Nigel Cattlin/Cumulus; p. **29** Terry
Heathcote/OSF.

Cover photograph of a dandelion bud, flower and seedhead by Alamy.

Some words are shown in bold, **like this**. You can find out what
they mean by looking in the glossary.

Contents

Nature's Patterns

Nature is always changing. Many of the changes that happen follow a **pattern.** This means that they happen over and over again.

Life cycles are patterns.

Plants make seeds that grow into new plants.

Plant life cycles follow a pattern. A **seed** grows, makes more seeds, and finally dies. Then the new seeds grow and make their own seeds. The cycle starts again.

New Plants

There are many different kinds of plants. But most of them grow in the same way. Most new plants have a life cycle that starts with a **seed.**

Seeds are made inside flowers. This tree has white flowers.

These seeds will grow into huge horse chestnut trees.

New plants **sprout** from seeds. Some plants grow very quickly. Other plants grow slowly. Trees are plants that can take many years to grow to their full size.

Growing Seeds

Most **seeds** grow in soil.
They start to grow into plants
under the soil. When a seed
starts to grow, this is called
germination.

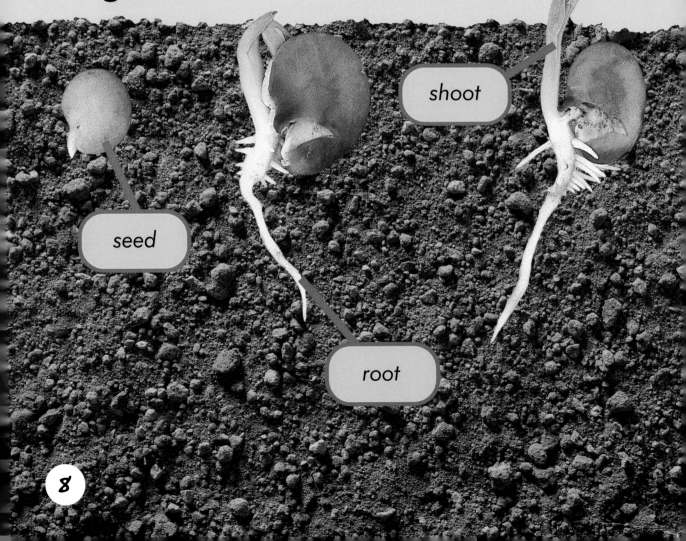

shoot

seed

root

First, the hard case around the seed breaks open. Then, a root grows down into the soil. A first shoot grows up and the plant's first leaves begin to open.

first leaves

A seed needs lots of water and sunlight to make it grow.

9

Rambling Roots

A plant's roots grow at the bottom of its **stem.** They are usually hidden under the soil. The roots hold the plant in place so that it does not blow over.

Some plants have thin, thread-like roots.

Trees have huge roots. You can see part of their roots above the ground.

As the roots grow, they get longer and spread out through the soil. There are tiny hairs at the end of each root. These hairs soak up water and **nutrients** from the soil.

Leaves and Food

Plants need food to live and grow. Animals must find food to eat, but plants can make their own. Plants make their food in their leaves. This is called **photosynthesis.**

Plant leaves open to face the Sun. Plants use sunlight to make their food.

A plant's leaves collect sunlight. They use it to mix **gas** from the air with water from the soil. Inside the leaves, the gas and water are turned into sugary food for the plant.

sunlight energy

A plant makes food from sunlight and water.

water taken up by roots

Strong Stems

A plant's leaves grow out of its **stem.** Some stems grow tall and strong. Other stems grow along the ground or curl around other plants for support.

The stem holds the plant's leaves up to the sunlight.

stem

There are lots of tiny tubes inside the stem. Some tubes carry water from the roots to the leaves. Other tubes carry food from the leaves all around the plant.

Tree trunks are stems that have grown very thick.

Blooming Flowers

Some plants grow flowers at the end of their **stems.** Other plants have flowers all along their stems. Flowers make **seeds** that grow into plants.

Many trees and plants grow their flowers in the spring.

bud

A rose flower grows from a rose bud.

A flower grows from a **bud.** Most buds are small and green. They burst open to show their flowers. Many plants flower in the spring and summer.

Inside a flower

There are many different parts inside a flower. These parts make the plant's **seeds.** One part of the flower makes a powdery dust called **pollen.**

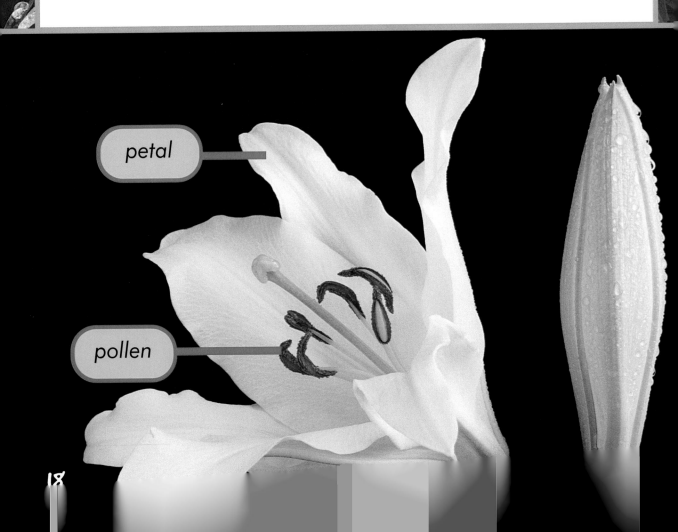

petal

pollen

Bees pick up pollen on their bodies and carry it to another flower.

Pollen travels from one flower to another. It joins with part of the new flower to make a seed. Sometimes the wind blows the pollen. Sometimes birds or insects carry it.

Sprouting Seeds

A **seed** starts to grow inside the flower. Once the flower has made a seed, its job is finished. Its petals **droop** and fall off, and the flower dies.

This rose has made its seeds. Now it droops and dies.

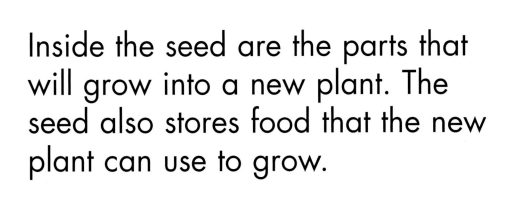

Inside the seed are the parts that will grow into a new plant. The seed also stores food that the new plant can use to grow.

There are lots of different parts inside a seed.

fruits and Nuts

Some kinds of **seeds** grow inside hard cases. When you crack open the hard shell of a walnut, you can see the seed inside. This seed is a nut you can eat.

The seed inside is a walnut. It is covered in a hard shell.

The seeds of an apple grow inside the fruit.

Some kinds of seeds grow inside juicy fruits, such as plums, cherries, and apples. Other seeds, such as peas and beans, grow inside cases called pods.

23

Scattering Seeds

Seeds need a good place to grow. Some seeds are so light that they blow away in the wind. Other seeds have tiny hooks that help them stick to animals' fur.

Dandelion seeds are so light the wind can blow them away.

When birds eat tasty berries, they also eat the seeds inside them. The seeds go through the birds' bodies. Then the seeds fall to the ground in the birds' **droppings.**

If seeds in the birds' droppings land in good soil, they start to grow and the life-cycle *pattern* begins again.

Growing from Bulbs

Some plants die in winter. All that is left of them are **bulbs** under the ground. A bulb is a ball of thick, fleshy leaves with roots and a short **stem.**

Onions are a kind of bulb.

In spring tulip flowers grow from tulip bulbs.

In spring bulbs **sprout** into new plants. The new plant uses the food stored inside the bulb to grow. In winter the plants will die down again.

Dying Down

Some plants, such as sunflowers, only grow one set of flowers and make one set of **seeds.** They flower in spring or summer. Then they die in fall or winter.

These sunflowers only live for a year, then they die.

Some trees can live for hundreds of years.

Some plants, such as trees, can live for many years. Each year, they grow new flowers and make new seeds. Others die down in winter but **sprout** again in spring.

How to Grow a Sunflower

1. Fill a pot with soil.
2. Make a hole, push the sunflower **seed** in, and cover it with soil.
3. Put your plant in a sunny place and water it often.

Glossary

bud start of a flower or leaf

bulb ball of thick, fleshy leaves with roots and a short stem

droop go soft

dropping solid waste from an animal

gas air-like material that is not solid or liquid

germination when a seed begins to grow

nutrient food that living things need to grow

pattern something that happens over and over again

photosynthesis how green plants make food from gas, water, and sunlight

pollen powdery dust in a flower

seed plant part from which a new plant grows

sprout start to grow

stem plant part that leaves grow from

More Books to Read

Carle, Eric. *The Tiny Seed*. New York: Aladdin Paperbacks, 2001.

Ganeri, Anita. *Living Things: Life Cycles*. Chicago: Heinemann Library, 2001.

Llewellyn, Claire. *Tree (Starting Life)*. Chanhassen, Minn.: NorthWord Press, 2004.

Index